SPIDER AND HIS SON FIND WISDOM

Obi nkyerekyere nyansa kotoku mfa nkɔto adakam mmegyina adihɔnse se, "Kyere me asem!"

No one should gather their wisdom in a bag, put it in a box, then stand on a road and say, "Teach me wisdom!"

Akan proverb

With thanks to Scott and Henry for sharing their nyansa and love.
—M.L.

For John, my wise son.
—C.R.

Spider and His Son Find Wisdom is based on "How Wisdom Became the Property of the Human Race," from *West African Folk-Tales*, by William H. Barker and Cecelia Sinclair. London: George G. Harrap & Company, 1917.

This tale is from the Asante and Fante peoples of the Akan culture of Ghana.

© 1998 The Rourke Press, Inc.

ILLUSTRATIONS © Charles Reasoner

Library of Congress Cataloging-in-Publication Data

Lilly, Melinda.
   Spider and his son find wisdom: [an Akan tale] / retold by Melinda Lilly; illustrated by Charles Reasoner.
      p. cm. — (African tales and myths)
   Summary: While trying to gather up all the wisdom he thinks he has wasted on the villagers, Ananse the spider learns something new himself.
      ISBN 1-57103-244-4
   [1. Anansi (Legendary character)—Folklore. 2. Akan (African people)—Folklore. 3. Folklore—Ghana.] I. Reasoner, Charles, ill. II. Title III. Series: Lilly, Melinda. African tales and myths.
PZ8.1.L468Sp 1998
[398.2'089'963385]—dc21   98–20334
                                                                                  CIP
                                                                                  AC

Printed in the USA

African Tales and Myths

SPIDER

AND HIS SON FIND WISDOM

An Akan Tale

Retold by
Melinda Lilly

Illustrated by
Charles Reasoner

The Rourke Press, Inc.
Vero Beach, Florida 32964

ong ago when the world was starting to learn about itself, there lived a spider named Ananse. He was a big headed spider who wove his sticky tricky webs across the villages of West Africa. He told everyone he was unusually big-headed for a spider because his head stored nyansa—all the wisdom in the world.

One day in the bustling marketplace, as he advised the weaver of the best patterns for kente cloth, he heard the rice seller and the millet farmer arguing nearby. Ananse hurried over to offer his wise counsel.

The rice farmer opened the bag of cooked rice sitting in front of him. "This is too much rice to trade for the little bit of millet grain you offer," he said.

"No, no, this is too much millet for the little bag of rice!" The millet seller piled her creamy white, cooked millet on a bright cloth. The two traders leaned toward each other, getting angrier with each word. They glared and waved their arms wildly! Their voices rose louder and louder.
Denden. DENDEN!

Ananse examined their wares. The cooked rice was plump and abundant. The heap of millet looked tasty. Ananse rubbed his small belly. Without calling attention to his wisdom, Ananse helped the rice farmer by eating some of his rice so there would no longer be too much. Then he helped the millet farmer by eating some of the extra millet.

Now, when the farmers noticed Ananse's wise deed, did they thank him? They did not. They chased him out of the marketplace!

Too clever to be caught, Ananse made webs connecting the thatched roofs of the village houses and sneaked out of town unnoticed. Then he raced for home.

anting, he leaned against the palm tree that towered over his family's small hut, shaking his head. How the farmers had mistreated him! People just didn't appreciate his nyansa. Ungrateful fools! Did they ever thank him for sharing his wisdom with them? For solving their problems? For spreading knowledge wherever he went? No! No! No!

Enough of being generous! Ananse decided. He would take back all the nyansa he'd given to the world. He'd put it in a calabash gourd and hide it at the top of his palm tree.

He looked across his family's farm. He watched his wife Aso working in her field of millet. He admired his son Ntikuma's field of calabash. It was green and vigorous, stuffed with gourds. Surely his young son wouldn't need to sell all of them at the market. Ananse saw Ntikuma poke his head up from behind a large calabash.

"Good morning, my son," Ananse said, smiling.

"Good morning, Father." Ntikuma glanced up from his weeding.

10

11

"Son," said Ananse, his eyes scanning the field, "I need a gourd to store my nyansa. So tell me, could you spare one of your calabashes?"

"Sure, Father," said Ntikuma, smiling. He jumped up and strode across the field whistling.

Ananse rested in the shade of the palm. Just as he began to doze off, Ntikuma returned. "Where's the—" began Ananse.

"Here's a gourd, Father." Ntikuma held out a tiny calabash.

"That runt?" exclaimed Ananse. "Why, that stunted thing couldn't even hold the millet farmer's smarts! Son, I need a big gourd." Ananse stretched out his many long legs, showing Ntikuma the enormous size of the desired gourd.

"I'll try to find one," said Ntikuma, getting his digging stick. He set off across the field.

"That's a calabash!" exclaimed Ananse when his son returned, rolling a giant golden gourd. "It's bigger than big. It's a kokuroo calabash!" Ananse thumped it happily. "Thanks, Son."

"You're welcome." Ntikuma pointed at the hole in the gourd where the thick stem had been connected. "How are you going to get wisdom in there?"

Ananse picked up a palm frond from the ground, saying, "I'll sweep up the wisdom I've scattered here and there, leaving it for fools. Then I'll put it inside."

"I've never seen wisdom before," said Ntikuma, bright-eyed. "May I come along as you sweep?"

"You see it every day, Son. You live with me! You just don't recognize it." Ananse sighed. "You bring the calabash, all right?"

14

15

nanse began by sweeping the family's one-room hut. He brushed under his bed, collecting wisdom that had fallen off of him while he dreamed. He swept under the table, picking up the snippets of genius that had dropped from his mouth during dinner conversation. He carried the palm frond outside, shook it in the opening of the gourd, and plugged the hole with a rag.

Next he cleaned the weedy area around the hut and brushed the twisting trail that led to the marketplace. Ntikuma followed behind, shoving, pulling, and rolling the unwieldy kokuroo calabash. "It looks nice where you've swept, Father," he huffed.

They followed the trail up a grassy hill to the village market. Wielding his palm frond, Ananse pushed his way between the tightly packed stalls and rushing shoppers. He quickly dusted between the heaps of fruits and vegetables, hoping to take back all the smart advice he'd offered so freely.

"Never seen you work before, Brother Ananse," said the weaver with surprise. "What's the occasion?"

Unwilling to risk sharing wisdom by speaking, Ananse simply waved his hand and moved on. He cleaned the entire market, but for the area where rice and millet were sold. He didn't want to save his knowledge of angry farmers chasing him.

As they left the village, Ananse swept the wide path that separated the thatched homes, collecting anything that might remain of the stories and jokes he'd told there. Then he helped Ntikuma roll the ungainly gourd back down the twisting trail. Father and son smiled as they trudged home, admiring the shiny world washed clean of wisdom. Everything gleamed. Even the dirt looked tidy.

21

When they reached the palm, Ntikuma pulled the rag out of the calabash and peered inside. "Wisdom looks a lot like dirt," he commented, disappointment in his voice.

"Of course, my son," answered Ananse. "All good things come from the soil of Africa. Wisdom is no different than rice or millet." Ananse wrapped a cord around the calabash. "Hold the gourd steady, will you, Son? I want to put in the nyansa that I've stored in my head."

Ntikuma wrapped his arms around as much of the gourd as he could. Ananse took a deep breath. He leaned over, putting his mouth over the opening in the calabash. Then he breathed his wisdom into the gourd. He blew and blew until his face turned purple. He puffed a final gasp of nyansa, and all his knowledge went in the calabash. He didn't have a wise thought left in his head.

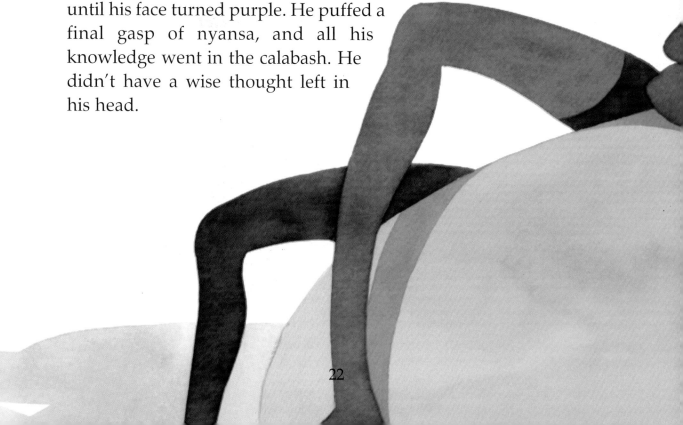

He quickly stuffed the rag in the hole before the wisdom could leak out. Then he looped the cord over his head and hung the kokuroo calabash in front of him. The weight of it made him wobble. Ntikuma steadied him and gave him a boost onto the palm.

Ananse began to climb very slowly. The big gourd stuck out so far in front of him that he could barely grip the smooth tree trunk.

"Father—" began Ntikuma.

"Not now, Son," Ananse barked. "I'm busy." He scooted slowly up the tree. The trunk became thinner and more slippery as he went up. Ananse held on by eight legs, then seven, six, five, four, three, two. When he was almost at the top, he dangled from a palm frond by one leg!

He swung and the calabash bumped him. *Pem so!* He fell down with a thud. *Paw!*

"Father, if you—" tried Ntikuma.

"Son, please, I'm trying to concentrate." Ananse struggled up the tree, then slid down. *Pem so paw!*

27

"The calabash, Father—" said Ntikuma.

Again Ananse went up and fell down. *Pem so paw!* Ntikuma helped his father up. "If you put the gourd on your back, you'll climb easily," he offered.

Ananse nodded and swung the gourd around. With it on his back, he easily scurried up the trunk. He sat at the top of the tree on a cushion of palm fronds, looking down at his son.

"Ntikuma is so young and already so smart!" Ananse shouted with pride. "I thought I carried all the nyansa of the world, but I didn't know how to carry the calabash. How could I have overlooked my son's wisdom?" Ananse took off the gourd, his head full of the new nyansa Ntikuma had taught him.

28

"No one can hoard all the wisdom of the world," Ananse yelled. He waved his son away from the palm tree. Then he pulled out the rag and tipped the kokuroo calabash off of the top of the tree. *Crash!* The gourd broke and wisdom escaped, scattered by the winds to all the homes and paths of the world. *Tetsee!*

Ananse has the last word:
"Ene se nyanse obiara nyaa bie, na wo a wanko ho ntem no, ene 'kwasea."
"That is how everyone got wisdom, and anyone who did not get there in time is—excuse my saying so—a fool."

31

PRONUNCIATION AND DEFINITION GUIDE:

Akan (AH kahn): A culture of Ghana.

Ananse (Ah NAHN´ seh): The main trickster of the Akan culture.

Aso (AH soh): Ananse's wife.

calabash (KAL´ uh BASH): A vine and its gourd.

denden (DEN DEN): Twi for loud.

kente (KEN teh): A handwoven regal cloth made by the Akan.

kokuroo (Koh KOO roo): Twi for huge.

Ntikuma (N tik OO´ mah): Ananse's son.

nyansa (Nie AHN sah): Twi for wisdom.

paw or **pɔw** (PAW): Twi word that means to bump.

pem so (PEM SOH): Twi expression that means to bump.

tetsee (tes EE): A descriptive sound.

Twi (CHWEE): Language of the Asante people of the Akan culture.